CW00434118

Dedicated to my own Little Dino. Alfinator, you are my inspiration and can bring a smile to the darkest of days. Keep being RAWSOME sweetheart, and remember you are perfect just the way you are.

Copyright © 2021 Amanda J. Flack

All rights reserved. This book or any portion thereof may not be reproduced or used in any manner whatsoever without the express written permission of the author except for the use of brief quotations in a book review.

Printed in the United Kingdom

First Printing, 2020
Second Edition 2021

ISBN: 9798553287948

This book belongs to

_____

LITTLE DINO'S
AUTASTIC GIFT

This Little Dino wasn't like all the rest,
He liked his home comforts
and stayed close to the nest.

Although small in size, his voice was colossal,
And all other RAAAWWS
made his ears turn to fossil.

His Mother would say
"Now go out and play",
But Little Dino didn't like the heat of the day.

His eyes would **burn**,
and his scales would sweat,
The sun was exhausting, making Little Dino fret.

Other Dino's his age
would play in the muck,
And listen to tales of The Greats and their luck.

But dirt gave this little Dino a **chill**,
And he'd never been able to sit very still.

When this Little Dino
asked to join in,
It sent other dinos into a spin.

For this Little Dino often got cross,
If he wasn't in charge, and known as **The Boss**.

At meal time Little Dino would retreat,
He did not like the look
of that **DINOSGUSTING** meat.

His Mother would say
"Come on, just eat one leaf",
But his stomach still churned
at the thought of that beef.

When it got dark, and other dinos were in bed,
A billion thoughts went through
Little Dino's head.

Like the FOSSILTASTIC smell of his favourite
berry brunch,
And how he didn't like sleep, or what
others like to munch.

When other dinos teased
and joked around,
This Little Dino would have a
Mighty Meltdown.

He knew it was wrong when his anger burned up,
But when it happened, he just couldn't let-up.

One day Mother decided
it was time,
She could see, quite clearly,
Little Dino wasn't fine.

See Mother had a **secret** she'd hidden
and locked away,
But she knew she had to tell him
before he went astray.

"All Dino's are different
in their own special way.
Some are strong; some are tall; some will slay;
some will play.

Your gift is called Autism.
Take pride in that fact,
Don't be afraid to make your impact."

"Your gift makes you truthful, logical and smart.
When routines throw you,
honour your kind heart.

Your **GIGANTIC** memory
will help you on your way,
And remember your smile
can brighten any dino's day."

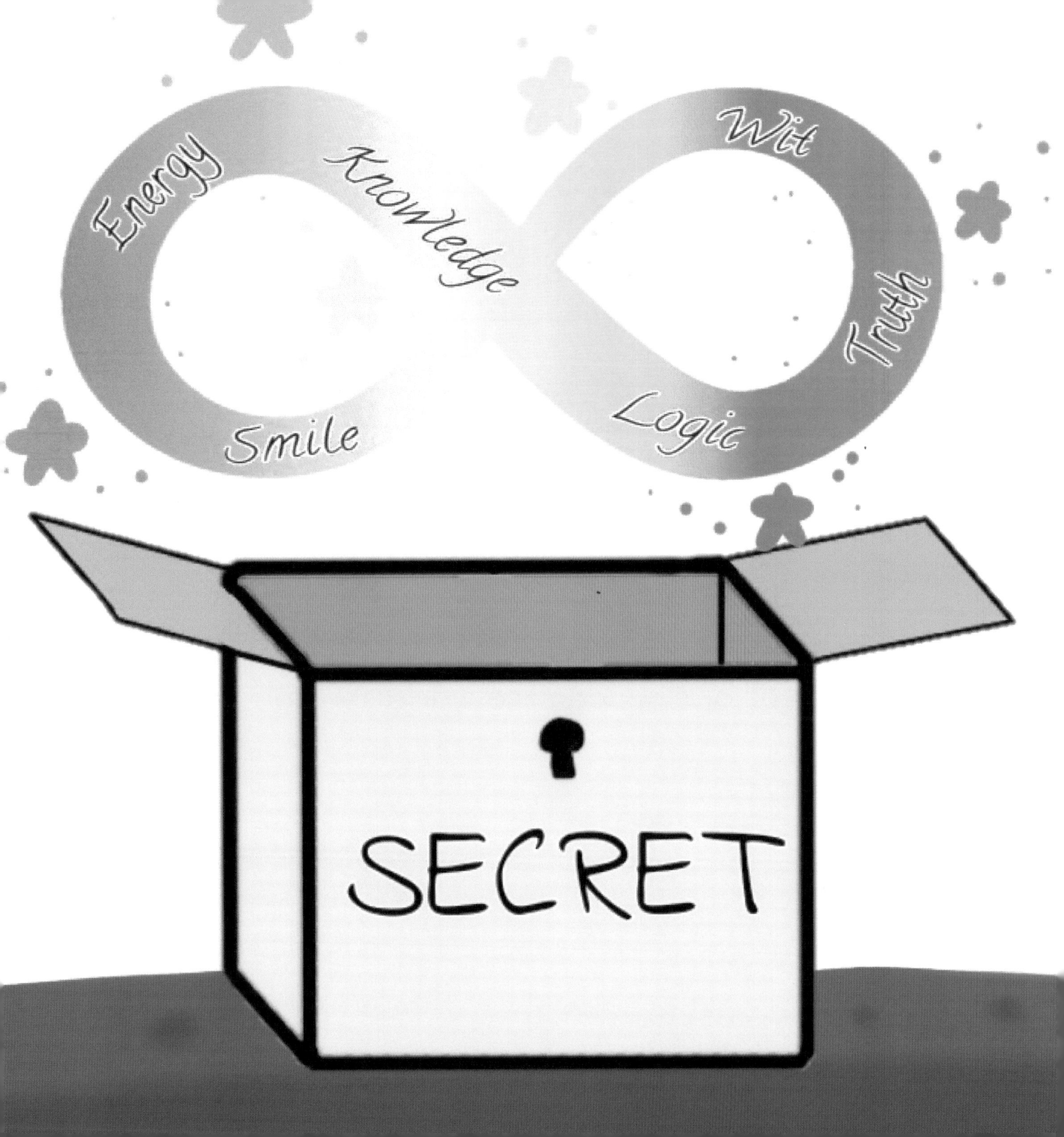
Energy
Knowledge
Wit
Truth
Logic
Smile
SECRET

Little Dino thought hard,
and then thought some more.
And after a while he realised the score.

He might be different
... but he had a **GIFT**!!!!
Then all of a sudden the world seemed to lift.

Little Dino had **POWERS**.
He could use them for good.
It didn't matter if he was a little misunderstood.

He was **RAAWWSOME**
and saw the world in a different light.
He could form a Super Dino Pack!
The future was bright!

From that day forward, life became **AUTASTIC**,
As he learnt to use his super senses,
energy and logic.

He realised his loudness
gave him even more command,
And he is now known as the most RAAWWSOME
dinosaur to ever walk the land.

Thanks

I am so grateful to the people who have helped make my dream a reality.

To my husband, for always being by my side through all the tough times and fun adventures. You are the very best of me, and my most perfect human.

To my daughter, for the thoughtful illustrations and all the lessons throughout this process! You fill me with pride. Your talent shines bright, and I know you will go far.

To Andrew and Heidi, for showing me the way and guiding me through the pits!

To my best friend, for always being there for me with belief and encouragement.

To all my family and friends, new and old, for your love and support.

I thank you from the depths of my soul x

Message From The Author

The Journey of Autism will be different for every child, but there are also common steps along the road to diagnosis. For a parent, getting that diagnosis can be fraught with conflict. A path with many obstacles and hurdles that results in parents having to armour up and fight for an outcome they don't really want. What I have taken from this journey is that the only expert you need to listen to wholeheartedly is your child.

I will never forget the system my son had to endure to get his formal diagnosis. After an "inconclusive" initial diagnosis and over three years of jumping through hoops, my son was finally diagnosed with ASD. Ironically, I didn't even know the appointment we were attending that day was a diagnosis meeting. Nevertheless, the diagnosis was given, and I was asked how I felt. I could hardly speak. Relieved that the palaver was over? Was that what she meant? Again the question came, how did I feel about my son now? Astounded to be asked that question! My amazing, smart, super savvy, gorgeous boy? Really? Why would that ever change?

Sitting in the car after the appointment, the pile of leaflets I had been given caught my eye. I had already planned how I was going to tell my son about the diagnosis, but I couldn't help but question why on earth there was not one leaflet aimed at my son? Not one piece of paper to help him understand the lifetime tag he had just been given. I guess this is when the "Little Dino's Autastic Gift" really began.

I do not profess to be an expert on autism of any kind. I am, however, an expert on loving my son, and for that reason, I will never again be left out in the corridor whilst others decide on the fate of my son. We parents walk the autism balancing act every day. We deal with fallouts, shutdowns, meltdowns, overloads, judgments, and requests upon request from various professionals. We also have the honour of raising these amazing children, that see the world in a refreshing way. That says it, exactly how it is. That brings the most wonderful joy to our lives with the simplest task."

About The Author

Amanda J. Flack grew up in Brighton alongside her younger disabled brother, who she describes as her guiding light. Her brother's death shaped her life and set her on a path to a career in the Disability Movement. Amanda met her husband whilst studying at University and has called Colchester her home, ever since. After finishing University, she worked for Essex Coalition of Disabled People (ECDP), where she campaigned for disability rights. Some of the changes achieved are still entrenched in U.K. equality laws. Amanda also played a fundamental part in a pioneering Post-Graduate Course for Disabled People at Anglia Ruskin University.

Amanda left ECDP to work as a freelance consultant when her daughter, the illustrator of *Little Dino's Autastic Gift*, was born. Her freelance work has been wide and varied, influencing equality for disabled people at a regional and national level. Amanda set up an Easy Read transcription service and is also frequently asked to consult on the accessibility of Health and Social Care documents.

Amanda's son was born and subsequently diagnosed with Autism. This led her to pursue her passion of working with disabled children. Amanda first taught at mainstream secondary level. Now she tutors disabled children who are out of school and awaiting placement.

Amanda believes education is not just an entitlement, but something that should be treasured. She thinks every child should have an equal learning opportunity, delivered in a way that is relevant and accessible to them.

Amanda has always enjoyed reading and writing. Some of her favorite authors include George Orwell and Lewis Carroll. Her message is that we could all benefit from a little bit more 'Wonderland' in our lives'!

Printed in Great Britain
by Amazon

35331016R00021